modern readers stage 3

The Turning Point

Veronica Teodorov

Richmond

© VERONICA TEODOROV, 2005

Richmond

Diretoria: *Paul Berry*
Gerência editorial: *Sandra Possas*
Coordenação de revisão: *Estevam Vieira Lédo Jr.*
Coordenação de produção gráfica: *André Monteiro, Maria de Lourdes Rodrigues*
Coordenação de produção industrial: *Wilson Troque*

Projeto editorial: *Kylie Mackin*

Edição e preparação de texto: *Kylie Mackin*
Assistência editorial: *Gabriela Peixoto Vilanova*
Revisão: *Maria Cecília Kinker Caliendo*
Projeto gráfico de miolo e capa: *Ricardo Van Steen Comunicações e Propaganda Ltda./Oliver Fuchs*
Edição de arte: *Christiane Borin*
Ilustrações de miolo e capa: *Cris Eich e Jean-Claude*
Diagramação: *Formato Comunicação*
Pré-impressão: *Hélio P. de Souza Filho, Marcio H. Kamoto*
Impressão e acabamento: Brasilform Editora e Ind. Gráfica
Lote 284738

Dados Internacionais de Catalogação na Publicação (CIP)
(Câmara Brasileira do Livro, SP, Brasil)

Teodorov, Veronica
    The turning point / Veronica Teodorov. —
São Paulo : Moderna, 2004. — (Modern readers ; stage 3)

    1. Inglês (Ensino fundamental) I. Título.
II. Série.

04-0932   CDD-372.652

Índices para catálogo sistemático:
1. Inglês : Ensino fundamental   372.652

ISBN 85-16-04090-9

Reprodução proibida. Art. 184 do Código Penal e Lei 9.610 de 19 de fevereiro de 1998.

Todos os direitos reservados.

RICHMOND
EDITORA MODERNA LTDA.
Rua Padre Adelino, 758 — Belenzinho
São Paulo — SP — Brasil — CEP 03303-904
www.richmond.com.br
2019

Impresso no Brasil

A good life

Hi there! I'm Eric and I'm going to tell you a story. It is about my life – my "other life". It was great. I lived in a wonderful apartment building, with a **huge** swimming pool, a soccer field, tennis **courts**, an enormous garden, and lots of nice **neighbors**. There was just one apartment on our floor, an entire floor just for me and my mom and dad. Oh...! I almost forgot Elizabeth, our **maid**. She lived with us too and just went home on weekends.

My father, William, is a **stockbroker**. He had a difficult **childhood**, but he studied a lot and got a good job at a big company. He met my mother, Helen, at a **company** party. She worked there too. It was **love at first sight**! They got married, moved to this apartment, and two years later, I was born. My mother **quit** working and stayed home **to take care** of me.

We had a nice life. Mom and Dad did lots of things together. They went to the supermarket, the shopping mall and the park. They always went to parties on weekends and I stayed home with Elizabeth. But very often, the three of us traveled together. We went to all kinds of **cool** places. But the best thing about our "old life" was shopping with my mother. She was so **trendy**. Once, my dad brought me back a jacket from the United States. He traveled there a lot **on business**. And can you believe it? Mom found the perfect pair of **sneakers** to **go with** it.

I liked the school I studied at. I had a lot of friends and the teachers were interested and smart. The school was in an **amazing** new building and it had a fantastic sports club. After school, my best friend Daniel and I usually spent the whole afternoon there. We played basketball, **sunbathed** or just talked and relaxed. But sometimes we met at my house. We did class projects together. Or we just talked about music, clothes and parties. On Sunday afternoons, we often went to **discos**.

One of the things I remember most about our past life was Mom's operation. She liked being in shape and **worked out** at the gym every day. But she still wasn't satisfied with her body, so she decided to have liposuction. My dad tried to make her **change her mind**, but she was determined to go ahead.

Mom went into hospital. Dad and I stayed with her the **whole time**. He brought her flowers and chocolates. But she just smiled and gave the chocolates to me. **After all**, her suffering had a reason. If she wanted to look good, she would have to **give up** sweets too. She had a slow **recovery**. And for some time, she didn't go to parties or shopping malls. My dad invited her to go out in the evenings, but she refused. She couldn't **even** drive her **powerful**, expensive car. She was in too much **pain**.

The first changes

Things started to change when I was 13. My dad started coming home late. And when he came in, he didn't want to talk to anyone. He **would** just give my mom a quick kiss and disappear into their room. When I asked Dad what was going on, he would just give me a **hug** and make an excuse.

As I told you before, we had a wonderful life. But soon, my dad became too ambitious. He started wanting to make more and more money. And then it happened. He invested our **savings** in a **risky** project and we lost almost everything. But the worst thing was not this. The worst thing was that he **hid** everything from Mom and me.

At least, I thought this was the worst thing. But **in reality**, this was just the beginning. Soon, Dad had to sell Mom's car. And we stopped **going away** so often. Now, Dad had to work **almost** every weekend. My parents also stopped going to parties and Mom **cut down** her trips to the shopping mall. She soon realized something bad was going to happen. When my dad finally told us the **truth**, it was too late. My mom was already **depressed** and I was really **angry**.

A new place to live

The weeks which followed were the most difficult for me. Remember our huge apartment? Well, we had to leave it and move to a much smaller one. In the new building, three other families lived on the same floor. It was strange opening the front door and seeing a **hall** with other doors.

It was a small building. There was no swimming pool or soccer **field**, just a **playground** for the little kids. But there was one thing I liked. The teenagers **hung out** on the **sidewalk**, in front of the building. I noticed this on the day we **moved in**.

The first thing I noticed about my new bedroom was its **size**. It was so **tiny**! And I had so much **stuff**!

"I'll have to keep some of my old things in Elizabeth's room," I thought. But then I remembered. She didn't have a room now. Our new apartment only had two bedrooms, a kitchen, a bathroom, and a small combined dining and living room. Elizabeth wasn't going to live with us anymore. We had to **cut expenses** now. She was just going to come in twice a week to help my mother.

Everyone felt really bad. Elizabeth had to find somewhere else to work. And another house to live in.

I was just **getting used** to my new apartment when I thought of something else – school. **Would** I have to change schools too? Well, I continued going to the same school I went to before we moved. But now, as I lived so far away, I had to walk back home. I didn't want to take a bus. I hated buses. And Dad couldn't drive me anymore because he was working too hard.

My friends didn't understand why I had to walk so far every day. I didn't **tell them the truth**. Instead, I told them I had to move because our apartment was being painted. But they kept asking me questions. My birthday was **coming up** and they started asking me about it.

When I talked to Dad about a party, he got **upset**.

"Eric, I **can't even afford** a present this year!"

"I'm not going back to that school then," I cried angrily.

"What's going on, Eric?" Dad asked.

"Everybody is asking me questions. I don't want to tell them that I'm not rich anymore!" I replied.

I stood up and went to my room. I slammed the door and my Dad **came after** me.

"Eric, open this door!" he shouted.

"No, I don't want to go to that school. I don't want to talk to those people." I cried. "I want my old life back!"

"Open the door and then we'll talk, son. I won't stand here at the door shouting all day long. Let's sit down and talk."

"I don't want to go to school anymore. Nevermore!" I shouted as I opened the door.

My dad sat beside me on the bed and we started talking. We talked for a long time. Dad told me that we all had to start a new life now, very different from the other one. He said we would all have to learn new things and **give up** other things. He said we should try to **make the most** of the situation. We decided that I should change schools and go to a private one near my house. It was as good as my old one but it wasn't so expensive.

Friends or acquaintances

After I talked to Dad, things seemed to **get better**. I tried to make the most of my new life. And I encouraged Mom to do the same. Soon, she was getting to know our new neighbors.

On the weekend, I didn't go out with my old **schoolfriends**. I wanted to relax. Monday was my first day at my new school. I wanted to be prepared. I was nervous, but I tried to **convince myself** that everything was going to be all right.

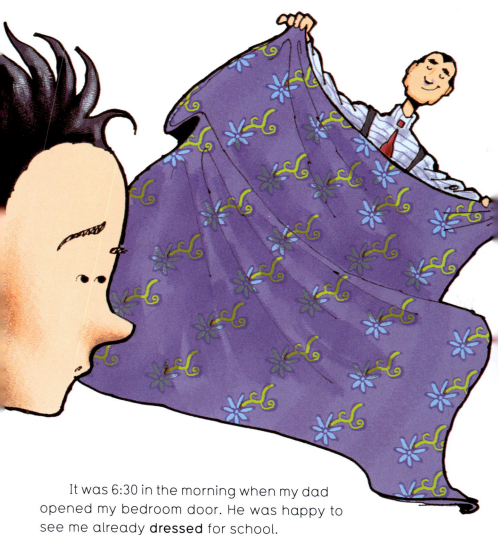

It was 6:30 in the morning when my dad opened my bedroom door. He was happy to see me already **dressed** for school.

"Hi son!"

"Oh, hi, Dad. I'm ready. Let's go."

"It's too early to leave for school, Eric. **In the meantime**, why don't you **make your bed**?"

"Make what?" I asked.

"Your bed, Eric. Don't you know how to make your bed? When I was your age, I made my bed every morning. Come on, I'll show you. It's really easy."

And it really was easy. From that day on, I made my bed every day.

Mom was **proud of** me. But in the beginning, Elizabeth was a little **jealous**. In the old days, she always made my bed for me.

One day, I was making my bed, when Elizabeth opened the door. She looked **upset**.

"Elizabeth, don't be **mad at** me. You know I have to do some things by myself now. You are not **around** all the time."

At 7:15, my dad drove me to school. When I arrived, I started feeling really nervous again. But I **hid** my feelings from Dad. I entered the school. All the other students looked at me. I found my classroom and waited for my teacher at the door. She arrived and **greeted** me with a smile.

"Hi, you must be Eric! I was **expecting** you. I'm your math teacher, Mrs Kawashi. Come in! Let's find you a desk!"

Mrs Kawashi introduced me to the class and told me where I should sit. Everything was going fine, but then I started thinking about the **break**. I was feeling anxious again. How would I **get along with** the other kids?

The **bell** rang... All the students stood up and left the room, but I stayed behind. I didn't know where to go or what to do. Suddenly, a boy appeared at the door.

"Aren't you coming?" he asked.

"I'm not hungry," I said. "And I don't know where I have to go."

"My name is Daniel. You can come with me if you like."

"Thanks. I'm Eric and it's my first day here."

"Yeah, I know. But I think I know you from **somewhere** else."

"From where?" I asked.

"Don't you live in that building, four blocks from here?" he asked.

"How did you know?" I asked.

"I live there too. I saw you when you moved in."

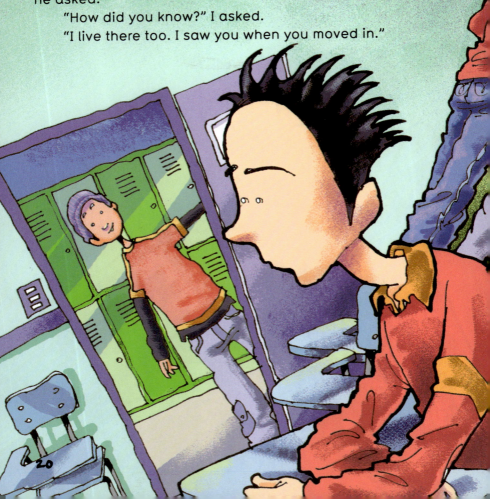

We went to the **schoolyard** and he introduced me to the rest of the group. Many of them lived in the same building as I did. They were all nice and friendly. There was a **pretty sixth grade** girl called Ana and a Japanese guy called Leo. Two of my other **classmates**, Arthur and Ivan, were kind of strange. Arthur had long black hair and wore **boots** with his school uniform. Ivan had six **earrings** and lots of **bracelets**. But he was a friendly guy and the girls seemed to like him a lot.

When we went back into class, I was feeling better. I now had some interesting new friends. And I knew I could talk to them without **lying**.

The **home bell** rang. I was on my way to the door when I heard someone calling my name.

"Eric!"

"Yeah, Daniel."

"Are you going home? If you are, why don't you come with us?"

"Sure. Let's go!"

I walked home with my new friends, talking and laughing. And we decided to meet up again in the afternoon.

A different story

When I got home, I told my mom about my first day. She was really happy that I had some new friends.

After lunch, Daniel rang our **doorbell**. We went **downstairs**. The rest of the group was there.

"Tell us about your old life, Eric!" said Daniel.

"Well, we lived in a huge apartment building. We had..."

And I went on to tell them all about what happened to my family.

When I finished, they asked me lots of questions.
"How do you like living here?" Ivan asked.
"Well, things are a **bit** strange. But I guess I'll **survive**," I said laughing. "To tell you the truth, I think I'm enjoying this life much more than the other one."
"Hey! Let's do something, guys! The soccer **field** is **crowded** today, but we could play here on the street. What do you think?" Leo asked.
"**Fine by me!**" said Ivan.
"OK!" said Daniel. "Are you coming, Eric?"
"Sure! If you want me to."

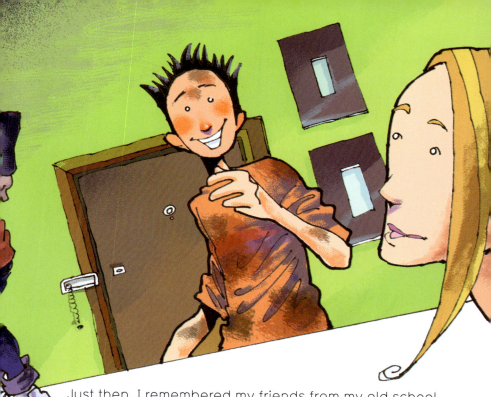

Just then, I remembered my friends from my old school. They only **worked out** at that **fancy** fitness center in the shopping mall. And the guys here seemed to have a lot of fun just playing soccer in the street.

When I got back home, it was almost time for dinner. I was dirty and **sweaty**. When my mom saw me, she couldn't believe her eyes.

"Eric, is that you?" she asked.

"Of course, Mom. Why? Do I look so different?"

"You sure do! What were you doing?"

"I was playing soccer in the street with my friends. My team won the game but we had to play **hard**. The other **team** is really good. And I **worked out** without going to the gym. You see! I saved us some more money."

Mom laughed. I was happy to see that her **sense of humor** was coming back.

My father arrived. And he was kind of shocked when he saw me too.

"Hi, Dad. Are you OK?" I asked.

"I am, Eric, but what happened to you?"

"Nothing, Dad. I was just playing soccer with my friends."

"It's good to know that you are **having fun**. I was worried about your first day at school.

"You don't need to worry, Dad. I made some great new friends. We played soccer and talked a lot. They are really **cool**."

"That's great news, Eric," he said.

A whole new Eric

In the beginning, I thought I couldn't live without the trendy, expensive clothes I wore in the old days. My father couldn't afford them anymore. But I started to pay attention to my friends' clothes. I realized they were very similar to those I wore in my "old" life. And they cost half the price.

Dad started giving us a little money each month and Mom and I went shopping at the mall, like we did in the old days. But now we walked a lot to check and compare prices. And we noticed how different they were. We could buy many things with the money Dad gave us because now we went to cheaper stores. Mom was very happy with all those shopping bags.

28

And so you see, all these changes didn't seem so bad **after all**. What was important was what my dad always said, "Try to **make the most of** the new situation!"

Oh, I forgot to tell you about the best change of all. Remember Ana? That **sixth grade** girl I met on my first day at school, the one who lives in the same building as I do? Well, now we are **getting to know** each other better. Almost every evening, we sit in the hall and talk for hours. With her, I am learning how to have fun without going to expensive restaurants, fancy parties and gyms. She showed me that the important thing is to **be myself** and not just **go along with** other people. And I can truly say that now I'm much happier than I was.

Well, my story ends here. Ana is waiting for me to go to the movies. Maybe another story is just beginning.

KEY WORDS

The meaning of each word corresponds to its use in the context of the story (see page number 00)

acquaintance (15) conhecido
almost (29) quase
amazing (6) maravilhoso
angry (11) bravo
around (18) por perto
bell (20) sinal
bit (24) pouco
boots (21) botas
bracelets (21) pulseiras
break (19) intervalo
childhood (4) infância
classmate (21) colega de classe
company (4) empresa
convince (16) convencer
cool (5) legal
court (3) quadra
crowded (24) cheio, com muita gente
depressed (11) deprimida
disco (6) danceteria
doorbell (23) campainha
dressed (17) vestido
earrings (21) brincos
even (8) mesmo
expect, expecting (19) esperar
fancy (25) chique
field (12) campo
greet, greeted (19) cumprimentar

hard (25) duro
hide, hid (10) esconder
hug (9) abraço
huge (3) enorme
hang out, hung out (12) encontrar-se
jealous (18) com ciúmes
just (3) apenas
keep, kept (13) guardar
lie, lying (22) mentir
mad at (18) brava com
maid (3) empregada
neighbor (3) vizinho
pain (8) dor
powerful (8) potente
pretty (21) bonita
proud of (18) ter orgulho de
quit (4) parar
recovery (8) recuperação
risky (10) arriscado
savings (10) economias
school friend (16) amigo de escola
schoolyard (21) pátio da escola
sidewalk (12) calçada
size (13) tamanho
slam, slammed (15) bater a porta
sneakers (5) tênis

somewhere (13) algum lugar
stockbroker (4) operador da bolsa de valores
stuff (13) tralhas
sunbath, sunbathed (6) tomar sol
survive (24) sobreviver
sweaty (25) suado
team (25) time
tiny (13) muito pequeno
trendy (5) na moda
truth (11) verdade
upset (18) chateada
worst (10) pior

Expressions

after all (8) afinal
at least (11) pelo menos
be myself (29) ser eu mesmo
being in shape (7) ficando em forma
best friend (6) melhor amigo
came after (15) veio atrás
can't even afford (15) não tem nem condições de comprar
change one's mind (7) mudar de idéia
coming up (14) chegando
cut down (11) cortou
cut expenses (13) cortar despesas
Fine by me! (24) Por mim tudo bem!

get along with (19) se relacionar com
get better (16) melhorar
getting to know (16) conhecendo
getting used to (14) se acostumando
give up (8) desistir
go along with (29) imitar
going away (11) viajar
go with (5) combinar com
having fun (26) se divertindo
home bell (22) sinal que indica término das aulas
in reality (11) na verdade
In the meantime (17) enquanto isso
kind of (21) meio
love at first sight (4) amor à primeira vista
make the most of (16) aproveitar ao máximo
moved in (12) mudamos
on business (5) a negócios
sense of humor (25) senso de humor
sixth grade (21) sétima série no Brasil
take care of (4) tomar conta de
the whole time (8) o tempo todo
went downstairs (23) descemos
worked out (25) malharam

ACTIVITIES

Before Reading
1. Look at the chapter headings and try to guess what is going to happen in each of them.

While Reading

A good life
2. Write the adjectives used to describe:

   the people   the building   the school
   _____   _____   _____
   _____   _____   _____

The first changes
3. Write T (True), F (False) or D (don't know).
   a) (   ) Helen knew what was happening to William.
   b) (   ) William sold Helen's car.
   c) (   ) Eric was depressed.

A new place to live
4. What were Eric's first impressions of the new place?

Friends or acquaintances?
5. What did Eric learn to do every morning? Do you do the same at home? Find someone in your class who does.

A different story
6. What does Eric think of his "new life" now?

A whole new Eric
7. Do you think Ana was important in Eric's new life? Why?

After Reading (Optional Activities)
8. Write down three things you can do without spending too much money. If they are for free, even better. Now, check what your classmates wrote and plan a "cheap, fun weekend" for the whole class.

32